Table of Contents

Photographs in this book show the life cycle of a humpback whale.

newborn

4

The Life Cycle of a

Whale

by Lisa Trumbauer

Consulting Editor: Gail Saunders-Smith, Ph.D.

Consultant: Ronald L. Rutowski, Professor,
Department of Biology, Arizona State University

Pebble Books

an imprint of Capstone Press
Mankato, Minnesota

Pebble Books are published by Capstone Press
1710 Roe Crest Drive, North Mankato, Minnesota 56003
www.capstonepub.com

Library of Congress Cataloging-in-Publication Data
Trumbauer, Lisa, 1963–
    The life cycle of a whale / by Lisa Trumbauer.
    p. cm.—(Life cycles)
    Includes bibliographical references (p. 23) and index.
    Summary: Simple text and photographs present the life cycle of the whale.
    ISBN 13: 978-0-7368-1186-6 (library binding)
    ISBN 10: 0-7368-1186-9 (library binding)
    ISBN 13: 978-0-7368-3398-1 (softcover pbk.)
    ISBN 10: 0-7368-3398-6 (softcover pbk.)
    1. Whales—Life cycles—Juvenile literature. [1. Whales.] I. Title. II. Life cycles
(Mankato, Minn.)
QL737.C4 T86 2002
599.5—dc21   2001004841

Note to Parents and Teachers

The Life Cycles series supports national science standards related to life science. This book describes and illustrates the life cycle of a humpback whale. The photographs support early readers in understanding the text. The repetition of words and phrases helps early readers learn new words. This book also introduces early readers to subject-specific vocabulary words, which are defined in the Words to Know section. Early readers may need assistance to read some words and to use the Table of Contents, Words to Know, Read More, Internet Sites, and Index/Word List sections of the book.

Printed in the United States of America in North Mankato, Minnesota.
062013
007346R

A whale begins life as a calf. A newborn calf can be the size of a small car.

calf

A mother whale takes care of her calf. She helps the calf get its first breath of air. The calf drinks milk from her body.

six months

The calf grows very
fast. It swims, plays,
and learns to live
in the ocean.

adult

The calf stays with
its mother for about
one year. It becomes
an adult. A whale
may live up to 50 years.

A male whale attracts
a female whale.
The two whales mate.

14

A calf grows inside
the female whale for
about one year.

Then the female whale
swims south to warmer
water. She is ready
to give birth.

The female whale
gives birth to a calf.

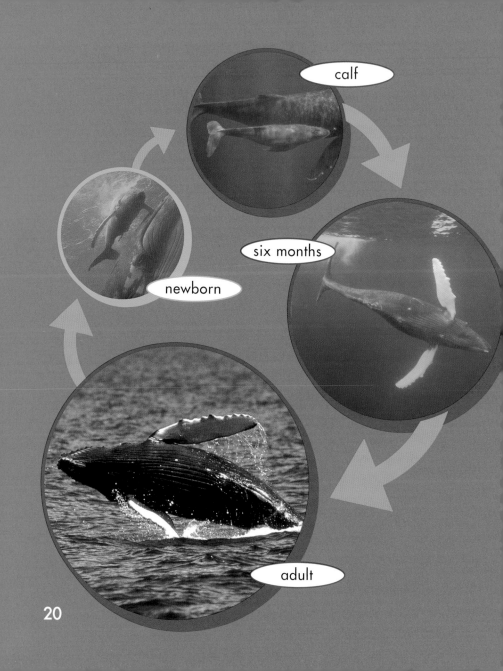

calf

newborn

six months

adult

The calf is the start
of a new life cycle.

(Words to Know

adult—an animal that is able to mate; most whales continue to grow after becoming adults; adult humpback whales can weigh up to 50 tons (45 metric tons).

attract—to get the attention of someone or something; when whales are attracted to each other, they move closer to one another.

breath—air that is taken in through the lungs and exhaled; whales breathe air through a blowhole on the top of their head.

calf—a young whale; humpback whale calves weigh about 2 tons (1.8 metric tons) at birth.

life cycle—the stages of being born, growing up, having young, and dying

mate—to join together to produce young

milk—a white liquid produced by the bodies of female mammals; female mammals feed milk to their young.

(Read More

Corrigan, Patricia. *Whales.* Our Wild World. Minnetonka, Minn.: NorthWord Press, 2001.

Kalman, Bobbie, and Heather Levigne. *What Is a Whale?* Science of Living Things. New York: Crabtree, 2000.

Rustad, Martha E. H. *Whales.* Ocean Life. Mankato, Minn.: Pebble Books, 2001.

(Internet Sites

FactHound offers a safe, fun way to find Internet sites related to this book. All of the sites on FactHound have been researched by our staff.

Here's all you do:

Visit *www.facthound.com*

FactHound will fetch the best sites for you!

Index/Word List

Word Count: 135
Early-Intervention Level: 16

Editorial Credits

Martha E. H. Rustad, editor; Jennifer Schonborn, production designer and interior illustrator; Kia Bielke, cover designer; Kimberly Danger, Mary Englar, and Jo Miller, photo researchers

Photo Credits

Amos Nachoum/Seapics.com, 4, 20 (left)
Dave B. Fleetham/Tom Stack and Associates, 6, 20 (top)
Doug Perrine/Seapics.com, cover, 8, 12, 20 (right). Taken under NMFS permits #633 and #882 issued to HWRF.
James D. Watt/Seapics.com, 18
Michael S. Nolan/Seapics.com, 10, 20 (bottom)
Paul A. Sutherland/Seapics.com, 1
Visuals Unlimited/Dave Fleetham, cover (inset); Gerald and Buff Corsi, 14; Hugh Rose, 16

Pebble Books thanks Jody Byrum for her assistance with this book.